THE DEAL

Annie Fisher

HAPPENSTANCE

ACKNOWLEDGMENTS:

Thanks to the editors of the following publications where some
of these poems first appeared: *Snakeskin*, *Obsessed With Pipework*,
Clear Poetry.

BY THE SAME AUTHOR:

Infinite in All Perfections (HappenStance, 2016)

Printed by The Dolphin Press
www.dolphinpress.co.uk

First published in 2020 by HappenStance Press,
21 Hatton Green, Glenrothes, Fife KY7 4SD
nell@happenstancepress.com
www.happenstancepress.com

CONTENTS

In Hiding / 5

Small / 6

The Fear / 7

The Gate / 8

Cold War Supper / 10

On Iona / 11

Perhaps / 12

His Face in My Mirror /13

Ghost / 14

Hotel Restaurant / 15

You Almost Said / 16

Picasso's Owl / 17

Cannibal / 18

Insurance Plan / 19

The Massacre /20

The Jungle Waits Outside, My Best Beloved / 22

Endurance / 23

The Orange Lobster and the Hens / 24

The Deal / 26

Naming This Place / 28

For S

IN HIDING

One day I climbed into the bedroom cupboard
hugged my knees and listened to the voices
the come and go of footsteps on the stairs

I stayed in there for years

hidden with the skeleton
they kept inside the cupboard
inside the little box room
inside the little house

where ten green bottles leaned against the wall
and my father popped out every night
to see a man about a dog

and my mother
who saw Christ in every soul
played nocturnes
on the out-of-tune piano in the hall

and they never heard me call

SMALL

How I envied the tall girls
sleek as swans
who glided
along corridors
while I scuttled
in their wake;
who could flip a netball
through a hoop
with a flick of a wrist
and both feet on the ground;
girls built to yawn and stretch
proud as cats;
who could look down
on Mr Tracey
and make him blush;
who never needed to try,
never needed to rush,
being already there
miles before me.
How I envied
the unearned prize
awarded to their size,
and when I looked
in the mirror
facing the limits
of my timid geography,
how I envied
the beautiful maps of their limbs
extending from Land's End
to distant ice-blond Arctic.

THE FEAR

Look, there's nothing to be scared of.

If there was something to be scared of
I'd be scared too, and I'm not.

So there's nothing to be scared of.

The only thing to be scared of is being scared.

So stop being scared.

If you go around saying you're scared
you'll make everyone scared.

Listen, there are known scary things,
unknown scary things and scary scary things.

I don't think about any of them.

There's no point being scared of what hasn't happened.
It might never happen. In fact, I know it won't happen
and that's why I'm not scared.

It won't happen because I've said it won't happen.
If I thought it would happen, of course I'd be scared.

But it won't.
So I'm not.

Stop talking about it.
I need you to stop.

THE GATE

Our bones were formed there
in the house of eleven secrets

in the garden
with its high white walls
and lime trees,
purple figs and vines
and a deep well
where we knew
a monster lived.

We bounced home
on the bus
down sun-bleached tracks
of limestone dust.
The leather seats burned
through our cotton dresses.
Pictures of virgin martyrs
rode the dashboard.

Then we played
under the lime tree
with our dolls
through the slow
siesta-silent afternoons

till Uncle Paul came
with red roses for our mother,
the darkest red,
the sweetest-ever scent.

He'd crook his yellow finger,
croaking foreign words
like some ancient
wrinkled frog
from down the well.

The eleventh secret was the gate—
how slow he'd open it.
We'd wait.
Jennifer must have been six,
I must have been eight.

COLD WAR SUPPER

In the days when reds slept under the dormitory beds
and infiltrated all our games, when we had code names
like Violette and Odette, and would gladly have died
singing Faith of our Fathers, I tasted pigeon
for the first and only time.

'Chew carefully girls,' Sister Ursula said with a wink,
doling out unctuous ladles of alien meat.
'Spit out anything hard; any nuggets or grit.'

We didn't ask. With our obedient tongues
we probed the tender flesh, all the more delicious
for being seasoned with conspiracy.

I see her now—as plump and reassuring
as a steamed pudding. She's stomping off to the woods
wearing boots and carrying a rifle.
She has forsaken (for the while)
all prayers for the conversion of Russia.
She means to shoot a brace of pigeon for our supper.

'Communists! Heretics!' she mutters.
'I can hear what you're plotting—A coup! A coup!
I'll give you something to coo about!'

ON IONA

Today, the ruined nunnery—
lichen and moss on slate and rock
and in the cracks these tiny lilac flowers.

In waterproofs and woolly hats
we peer through mizzling rain
as if we could recover faith from stone

or glimpse the dead who once belonged to us
or paler, distant ghosts we fear to lose
receding like the white sand and the sea

and the dolphins we saw leaping yesterday
surging through the Sound, so close
beside our boat we almost touched.

PERHAPS

I stood by the ocean.
I wanted to understand love.

I remembered a man.
I remembered a girl,

a small girl who clung to her father's white back
as he swam over green-bottle depths to a rock.

The father who knew how to swim
and the girl who could not.

> *Ten green bottles sitting on a wall*
> sang the man (who was drunk)

> *And if one green bottle should accidentally fall?*
> sang the girl (who was not)

Was that love? I asked the ghost of the man.
I cannot speak about love, said the man
(he could not).

Was that love?
I called to the ocean.

Perhaps it was love—
said a wave as it washed my white feet—
then again, perhaps not.

HIS FACE IN MY MIRROR

The little lazy eye he gave to me
Winks back unmistakably.
Try all you like, it seems to say
You can't escape your DNA.

GHOST

She's weighed herself again.
She's six stone three
and finds this satisfactory.
Tonight she'll have
two eggs (hardboiled)
one orange
and a cup of tea.

Midsummer
and she's sitting on
the college lawn
a notepad on her knee.
He's told them to *Enjoy the sun.*
Write anything. Come back at four.
But she can't write at all.

The page gapes
like an empty plate.
She tries to calculate
the calories in birdsong
the fat and carbohydrate
in a flower. She watches
as her shadow on the ground
grows more obese
with every passing hour.

HOTEL RESTAURANT

The males will squat for hours
on these padded leather chairs:
round-bellied corporate frogs
dispatching coffee and Full English
with their long elastic tongues

and here two Saga iguanas
too old for noise or rush
are lipping sweet, stewed fruit
and honeyed yogurt
from the tips of trembling spoons

while sad-eyed at his single table
sits the walrus man
(koo-koo-kachoo)
his poached egg smiling for him
like a little yellow sun.

YOU ALMOST SAID

I loved our babies achingly when they were fast asleep.
I had to know, of course, that they
were breathing properly, but once
I'd checked they were OK
I had the time to love them in a way
that never quite seemed possible
when they were wide awake.

Lately I've been waking early (must be age)
and listening to snores that would have driven
weaker spouses out the door. Sometimes
though, it all goes quiet; your flow
of breath's nearly inaudible, and then
I have to rest my hand across your chest
to feel your heart and know that you're alive.

It's something like that aching love again,
although I'd never say. It isn't what we do.
Through the window I can see the April light,
the two beech trees. What was it Larkin wrote?
The trees are coming into leaf
Like something almost being said.

I used to ask you
if you loved me.
You always said
'Taken as read.'

PICASSO'S OWL

It wakes for food,
staring at him hard.
Gloss black eyes
in the clock
of its face.
The hour is now
in its egg belly.
He feeds it
mouse.

It clamps the tail
in its beak,
swinging
the corpse
like a
pendulum.
Three
gulps
and it's gone.

He paints it
on pitcher,
plate and canvas.
Its eyes
are watching him.
Cochon-merde!
They are his eyes
but unafraid
of time.

CANNIBAL

When I opened the door of the fridge
the bunch of green grapes I'd placed on the top shelf
was eating the blue grapes on the shelf beneath,

a feat of relocation I presumed it had achieved
by animating its pale stems, then lurching,
triffid-style, towards the edge

from whence, impelled by ravenous intent,
it must have flung itself so that the whole bunch tumbled down
to land in one pulsating clump upon the lower ledge

whereupon each green grape (I surmised)
had split its skin, creating slit-like mouths which feasted
monstrously upon the wretched blues.

And all that day the horror stayed with me.
I saw the blue grapes' innocence, their bloom—
I saw the way the green grapes drooled

and how the rest of them—the mince,
the eggs, the ham, the chicken thighs—
played dead.

INSURANCE PLAN

Weaned too soon, he learned right from the start
life would be a disappointing game.
His Airfix models always fell apart
as soon as glued. He understood this shame
as his trajectory, God's chosen scheme.
Let-downs ambushed him throughout his life—
the taste of fresh-perked coffee; aubergines;
live albums; picnics; Camembert; his wife.

Each day was guaranteed to break its promise.
Had things been otherwise it would have felt
all wrong. His one hope? Not to be astonished.
He trusted every ice-cream cone would melt
just as it did, and thus he was protected.
His epitaph read: *Much as I suspected.*

THE MASSACRE

Two stops up from Pimlico
and one past Rochester Row
the automated voice always announced
the bus stop's name as *Meathouse Place*.

She definitely said it. Every time.
Or that was how I heard it said.
I always felt a shiver down the spine
when the 185 stopped there.

I pictured dim-lit rooms
and butchery.
I saw the blood, the gleaming blade.
I heard the screams.

When I realised the voice
was saying *Neathouse*, not *Meathouse*,
I tried to swap the crimson nightmare
for a plain vanilla dream.

I binned the knives and washed the surfaces.
I sprayed everything with Mr Sheen.
I conjured up a white-starched parlour maid,
a glowing fire, a hearthrug and a cat.

But 'scenes some viewers may find'
defile the mind indelibly.

In Neathouse Place there still remains
a faint stain on the polished floorboards
and the cat has gouged the table
with her unretractable claws.

THE JUNGLE WAITS OUTSIDE, MY BEST BELOVED

Another zoo, another information board,
another wild encounter talk. I'm old

and neurotypical. The facts and stats
glide through my head and out the other side.

You, on the other hand, remember everything.
Your nine-year-old, extraordinary mind

could itemise, if asked, the eighty-five names
humankind has given to the Puma.

At the end of our day out, you asked what animal
I loved the most in Exmoor Zoo and I said—*Guess*.

You thought perhaps the Binturong
(which smells, you said, like popcorn) or judging by

my oohs and aahs, maybe the Superb Starling,
the Scarlet Ibis, or the gloriously grumpy Tawny Frogmouth.

When I said, No, *YOU are my favourite animal*, I knew
I'd disappointed you. The look that flashed across your face

told me I'd made a category mistake.
But later you said, *Thanks Grannie. Today has been the best.*

And yes it was. We were so safe among the cages.

ENDURANCE

endure	*endure*
it's a strange word	for sure
beginning with	*end*
endure	*endure*
as in heartache	or pain
as in *to bear*	(remain)
as in *to weather*	and *forever and forever*
endure	*endure*
as in *survive*	(abide)
as in *prevail*	(persist)
as in *to be*	as in *it is like this*
endure	*endure*
as in *to tolerate*	(and wait
to know)	*to undergo*
as in *to last*	hold fast
this too will pass	*this too will pass*

THE ORANGE LOBSTER AND THE HENS*

I was reading *The Loneliness of Donald Trump* by Rebecca Solnit
on the last train out of Temple Meads. I was up to
the bit where it says: 'He was a pair of ragged
orange claws, forever scuttling, pinching, reaching
for more'—when the automatic toilet door
sighed open for the umpteenth time,
releasing the repugnant, chemical smell
that marks all toilets on trains these days.
Not that I was complaining. I'd grabbed
the last priority seat, well-placed to enjoy
the in-coach entertainment provided by
a nine-strong hen party who did a sort of
relay to and from the loo on kitten heels.
I gave up reading when the singing started:
If I could turn back ti-ime! If I could find a way-ay!
It was loud, but non-threatening. Next came
Bohemian Rhapsody. *Mama! Just killed a man!*
they wailed in generous sliding tones, liberating
Freddie's masterpiece from its intended keys.
I wanted to sing too—was just about to start
when the orange lobster twitched inside
the pages of my book and suddenly broke free.
It scuttled across to where they sat
and clambered onto one girl's foot,
where it was doused with a can of Thatcher's Gold
and set upon with handbags.
The lonely lobster, bruised and soaked,
groped blindly, reddening and puffing up
until at last its carapace exploded to create
a bright mosaic sunset on the carriage floor.

The girls, all pink and orange glow, broke into song again.
They sang on, long and loud, all the way to Bridgwater.
Go on now, go! Walk out the door
Just turn around now
Cos you're not welcome anymore!
I almost loved my town that night.
I almost thought it could be great again.

---

* A female lobster is known as a 'hen'.

THE DEAL

When I knew I was going to die
I walked up to the church in Easter sun,
past people shut inside
their quiet afternoons.

The church was locked
so I sat down
in the shade
and did a deal with God.

Daffodils bloomed everywhere.
Ridiculous
their born-again belief
in bulb and bud, in flower and leaf.

I walked among the graves
reading out the names
of those who'd died
before the age of sixty-five

and part of me looked down
on all of this—the vivid yellows
and sad greys, the little figure
moving through the graves.

I watched her walk back home
over the fields and stiles
clutching her wilting bunch
of promises and prayers.

Five years on (the daffodils
and symptoms both long gone)
I'm hazy on the details
of that afternoon.

Who promised what exactly?
And to whom?

NAMING THIS PLACE

This garden's called *The Sweet Relief of Silence*
and the sky is called *A Sleepiness of Weather*.
Those tumbling, purple blooms are called *Probably Roses*
and the small yellow flower on the trellis is called
Momentary Chink of Bright Sunlight.
This poppy's called *Old Woman in Red Petticoats*.
That shady corner's called *Refuge of Rabbits*.
This unmown patch of grass is called *The Universe*.